NATIONAL GEOGRAPHIC

Ladders

MANY CULTURES

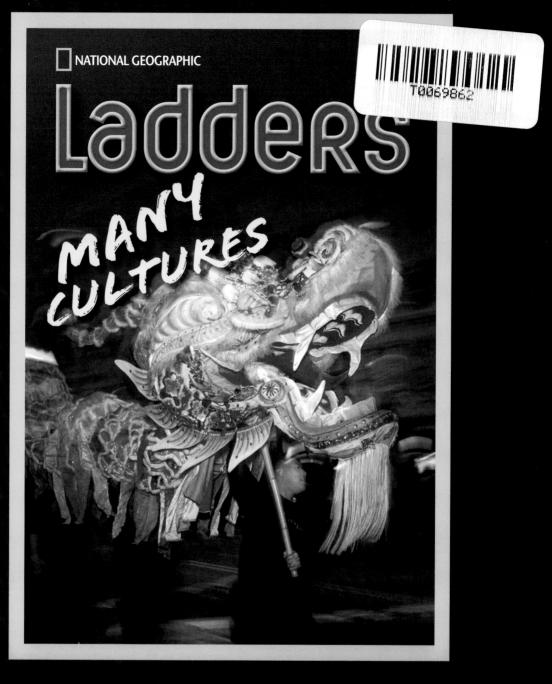

A Nation of Many

The United States is a nation of many cultures. Except for Native Americans, everyone in the country is an **immigrant** or descended from an immigrant.

Before the United States became a nation, people from many European countries settled here. And then later, more people arrived from Asia and Latin America.

Cultures

by John Manos

Immigrants left their homes and made the difficult journey to the United States for many reasons. Some came unwillingly as slaves from Africa and the West Indies. Some were persecuted in their homelands. Many came hoping to own land, while others came in search of work. Almost every willing immigrant came to America in hopes of a better life.

This desire still drives immigrants who come to America today. Every year people arrive from Mexico, Central America, Canada, India, Korea, and many other places. The mix of cultures and **ancestries** has made the United States an exciting, innovative nation.

Leaving Home

Throughout history, the United States has experienced waves of different groups of immigrants at different times. For example, in the late 1800s and early 1900s many Europeans from the Russian Empire, Sweden, Norway, and Ireland arrived at Ellis Island in New York. Throughout the 20th century and into the 21st century, more United States immigrants have come from Mexico and countries in Asia and Latin America. More recent waves of immigrants often entered by way of California on the west coast, instead of New York on the east coast of the United States.

Global events such as conflicts, natural disasters, or economic hardships in people's native countries have caused large populations of immigrants from all over the world to leave their native countries and move to the United States. In the 1840s and 1850s, more than a million Irish came to the United States to escape a devastating famine in Ireland.

U.S. and Foreign Born Population

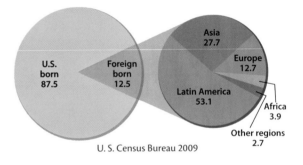

U.S. born 87.5

Foreign born 12.5

Asia 27.7

Europe 12.7

Latin America 53.1

Africa 3.9

Other regions 2.7

U. S. Census Bureau 2009

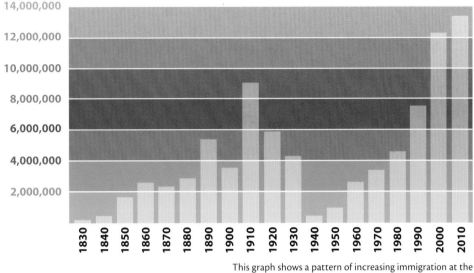

U.S. Immigration by Decade

This graph shows a pattern of increasing immigration at the end of the 20th century and beginning of the 21st century.

Immigrants from Germany and England also arrived as their nations faced changes. And in the 1850s in San Francisco, California, Chinese immigrants began arriving, too.

Historians chart the peaks and valleys of immigration to the United States. The greatest peak in immigration during the 1900s came in the first decade. Many United States citizens today can trace their family **heritage** to immigrants who arrived during this time period. Recent statistics show a shift in immigrant population. Today

12% of the United States population is made up of immigrants. Over half of today's immigrants are from countries such as El Salvador, Cuba, Guatemala, and Mexico. More than 25% of immigrants come from Asian countries such as the Philippines, Korea, Vietnam, and India.

Presently there are over 300 languages spoken in the United States. After English, according to census statistics, Spanish, Chinese, French, German, Tagalog, Vietnamese, and Italian are the languages with the most speakers.

Festivals

People who come to the United States from other countries bring their own long-standing traditions with them. That is one of the many ways immigrants maintain their culture. At the same time, their traditions enrich the culture of their new home. A variety of traditions become part of the fascinating cultural mosaic that makes up the United States.

Tet Festival - Vietnamese

Tet is the most important holiday in the Vietnamese culture. Tet occurs sometime from late January to early February every year. Annually, Californians of Vietnamese ancestry living in San Jose host a Tet festival, which includes a parade with dancers.

Chinese New Year Festival

For more than 5,000 years, the New Year has been celebrated in the spring in China. As Chinese immigrants settled in San Francisco beginning in the 1860s, they brought the holiday celebration with them. Today the festival includes the Chinese New Year Flower Fair and the Chinatown Community Street Fair. The highlight is the Chinese New Year Parade. Many consider it one of the world's best parades. Beautiful floats and amazing costumes pass by, ending with the Golden Dragon. It is over 200 feet long and is carried by more than 100 men and women. As the dragon moves slowly along, 600,000 firecrackers explode alongside it!

Arab International Festival

Immigrants of Arab heritage come from the Middle East. In Dearborn, Michigan, the Arab International Festival hosts more than 300,000 people from all over the United States and Canada. The street festival is filled with music, dancing, entertainment, and delicious food.

Dragon Festival - Hmong

Hmong immigrants come from Laos and Vietnam. St. Paul, Minnesota has the largest population of Hmong immigrants in the United States. A festival takes place in St. Paul every summer and includes dancing, food, and a soccer tournament.

The Arts

Americans enjoy many benefits living in a nation of immigrants. One benefit is the richness of the cultural traditions that are everywhere in the country—as newcomers arrive, they bring traditions from their cultures, such as music and dance.

Immigrant traditions influence the arts in the United States. The traditions of immigrants often take new directions in a new place and people of all backgrounds learn to participate in the artistic expressions of culture.

Dance

The polka dance comes from the region that is now the country of the Czech Republic and Poland. A fast, lively dance, it is the basis for several American dances. Many European, Latin American, and African traditional dances have influenced American dance styles and trends, as well.

Music

Instruments, songs, and rhythms from African and Latin countries came to the United States with immigrants both willing and unwilling. Many of the first Africans living in the United States lived as slaves. Over time, elements of African music traditions and Latin musical traditions found their way into new music genres that are characteristically American—jazz and blues.

Cuisine

Foods come in all shapes and sizes including some small packages, such as empanadas, perogi, and spring rolls. Delicious food is almost everyone's favorite cultural connection. Each new immigrant group arriving in the United States brings with it delicious foods that people from other backgrounds have often never tasted. Immigrants bring recipes from their countries of origin. Today many grocery stores and farmer's markets stock international fruits, vegetables, and spices to help people prepare traditional meals of many cultures from around the globe.

New Staples

In the United States, people have long enjoyed different kinds of bread, rice, and potatoes. For some, these foods are staples of many meals. When different immigrant groups arrived, people added tortillas from Mexico and Central America, pitas from the Middle East, and naan (or nan) from India to their plates. Which ones have you tried?

This woman is working with dough.

Food Trucks

Nothing beats the ability to find delicious food to eat on the go. But tasting food from cultures around the world makes it even better. From New York to Hawaii, food trucks await customers on busy corners. Whether you want shrimp tacos, Korean barbecue, or Cuban fried plantains, it's out there on wheels!

Just as foods from all over the world have made eating more interesting in the United States, ethnic festivals and the arts make all aspects of life in the United States ripe for adventure. So seek out something new and find a festival or new food to enjoy!

Check In What is one way immigrant groups influence life in the United States?

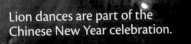

Lion dances are part of the Chinese New Year celebration.

12

LION DANCES AND DIM SUM

by Alexandra Behr

Baby Eli and his mom in a Chinese hotel, 2005.

Eli dressing up at his Mandarin preschool, 2008.

In 2004, a healthy baby boy was left at an orphanage gate in China. He was about seventeen days old, but had no note on him telling about his biological parents (also called "birth parents"). My husband and I adopted this little baby in 2005, when he was ten months old. We kept his Chinese name, *Zheng*, and gave him the first name *Eli*. Not knowing his birth parents is an emotional loss for Eli, but we're sure they loved him very much! Eli has no way of knowing how he is like them—whether he inherited his birth mother's laugh or his birth father's eyes. As a result, we help him feel proud of his origins in other ways. We believe families formed through adoption should help their children form connections with their cultural **heritage** so they feel proud of their background.

Adoption experts state that adopted kids become secure by understanding their **cultural identity**. Eli spent nearly a year in an orphanage in Chongqing, China, which is by the famous Yangtze River. Consequently, we have talked about China and Chinese culture since he was very young. We celebrate Chinese New Year at his school and attend Chinese American events. Eli even went to a Mandarin preschool. Mandarin is the official language in China. While there, he learned Chinese traditions, including songs in Mandarin.

Mountains edge the Yangtze River.

According to child psychologists, six- to eight-year-olds start to question who they are in the world. If they are adopted, they may wonder how they are similar to their birth parents. Since we do not know Eli's birth parents, we support his pride in being Chinese American. Right now, Eli is a second grader in Oregon, and he likes to play four square and tell jokes. For a class assignment, each student explained why he or she was important. Eli could have told about being athletic or funny, but he answered, "I am important because I am Chinese." This suggests he has a strong cultural identity.

We want to visit Eli's orphanage again to cement his connection to China. For example, in the book *Kids Like Me in China*, an adopted girl travels from her home in California to her Chinese orphanage. She states, "China isn't my home anymore, but it's where I was born. . . . It's good to know there are so many kids like me there."

As Eli reaches the ages between nine and twelve, his interests may change from playing four square to skateboarding. His feelings about his personal history may change, too. Child experts state that when children enter fifth grade, they want to fit in even more with other kids, and as a result, Eli may not want to answer questions about his heritage. He may want to keep his adoption story private. However, his dad and I believe that the more he loves himself for who he is, the more he will be able to tackle challenges that come his way.

The Great Wall of China—Eli would like to build one in our back yard!

Dim sum is a style of Chinese food. Eli loves his spicy!

正

strong and honorable

The Chinese symbol for Zheng means strong and honorable.

Portland, Oregon's Lan Su
Chinese Garden

Check In How is Chinese culture a part of Eli's life in the United States?

Tricksters Everywhere You Turn

Folk tales retold by John Manos | illustrated by Amanda Hall

Mischief in Every Culture

In the folk tales of virtually every country you will find a "**trickster.**" The story line of the tricky character who wins by using his or her wits seems to appeal to all people, no matter where they are, and this folk **motif,** or recurring central idea, unites all cultures. It's almost as if trickery and mischief are essential to our common human **heritage.**

By tradition, the trickster is typically a male animal of some kind, but he may be human or almost human. In Japan, he might be Kitsune, the fox, or Tanuki, the "raccoon dog." In Southeast Asia, the trickster is a mouse deer. Iktomi is a spider among the Lakota of North America. The trickster is Coyote in the folk tale traditions of many other Native American peoples. In West Africa, Anansi the spider is a trickster, and so is a tortoise, while in southern Africa near the Sahara Desert the role is played by a praying mantis. The trickster in India is frequently a monkey. The list goes on and on.

Mouse Deer from Southeast Asia

Tricksters are sometimes funny and mischievous and other times mean and devious, plotting to win or **outwit** no matter the cost to the other characters in the tale. Many trickster animal characters are smaller than the other characters that appear in the stories with them. Almost all of the tricksters survive by their wits; they trick other animals without mercy. And sometimes they get caught. Most often, though, the tricksters get away with their tricks.

Mantis from the African Sahara

Coyote from the Maya of Central America

Tanuki from Japan

Anansi the Spider from Ghana

Iktomi Spider of the Lakota in North America

Monkey Crosses the River

Monkey is a famous trickster in India and a monkey character in the trickster motif makes sense, since real monkeys are tricky pests in some parts of the country. In the folk tales, Monkey often tricks Crocodile, who wants to eat Monkey.

Crocodile watched Monkey hop from rock to rock to get across the river to eat from the large fruit tree. Crocodile had a plan to catch Monkey—he would pretend to be a rock!

Monkey was hopping across the river when he noticed that one rock was much larger than he remembered. Realizing immediately what was happening, he decided to outwit Crocodile once again.

"Hello, Rock!" Monkey cried out, but of course there was no answer. Monkey called out again, but again there was no answer, so he pretended to think out loud, saying, "That's odd! Why won't my rock talk to me today? I hope everything is all right!"

This led Crocodile to conclude that Monkey actually talks with rocks, and he thought, "I'd better answer if Monkey calls out again."

When Monkey greeted the rock once more, Crocodile answered, "Hello, Monkey!"

Monkey fought down a laugh and asked, "Crocodile, is that you lying on top of my rock?"

"Yes," Crocodile answered sheepishly, adding, "come a little closer so I can eat you!"

"I guess I have no chance," Monkey sighed. "Open your mouth wide, and I'll just jump in." Monkey smiled, knowing that when a crocodile opens its mouth very wide, its eyes close. When Crocodile did as Monkey suggested, Monkey leaped over his jaws and onto his back, then leaped across the river to the fruit tree.

Crocodile groaned unhappily, knowing that Monkey would always be too clever for him.

Compère Lapin Clears the Field

West Africans from Nigeria tell tales of Zomo the Rabbit. When West Africans came to the Caribbean, the rabbit character became Compère Lapin. Compère means "accomplice," or partner in French. Lapin is French for "rabbit."

Compère Lapin wanted to get married, but by tradition other rabbits refused to marry anyone who was not farming a good plot of land. Compère Lapin was far too lazy to clear a field in order to impress a potential bride, so he tried to think of a way to get a field cleared without having to work at it.

As he walked along, he happened to meet Ox and seeing the large, powerful animal, Compère Lapin had an idea. "Ox!" he shouted, grinning as if they were the best of friends, "I know you are strong, but I believe I am stronger."

Ox snorted and demanded that Compère Lapin prove it. "I will," Compère Lapin declared, handing the end of a long rope to Ox. "When I tell you to, pull with all your might," Compère Lapin said, "and we will see who is stronger." Then he ran off, carrying the other end of the rope.

Compère Lapin pulled the rope across a field until he found Horse. As he did with Ox, Compère Lapin issued a challenge, which Horse accepted and gripped the other end of the rope. Compère Lapin ran halfway between Horse and Ox and called out, "Now! Pull with all your might!"

As the two powerful animals pulled against each other, Compère Lapin guided the rope back and forth across the field in order to clear it. Once all of the work was done, Compère Lapin went to each animal and sighed in Creole, "Mwen lage," or "I give up." But in addition, he flattered each animal saying that each was the stronger animal, much stronger than Compère Lapin. Horse and Ox went home to dinner, each well pleased with his strength, while Compère Lapin smiled at his cleared field and put on his best clothes so he could begin his search for a bride.

Juan Pusong and the King's Field

Some tricksters appear as humans. Many tales of the trickster Juan Pusong are told among Filipinos. Juan Pusong is most often shown as a boy or young man.

On the island of Luzon there lived a boy named Juan Pusong, or "Tricky John," and as his name suggests, Pusong played many tricks on people.

Once he decided to trick the king. He crept into the field where the king's cows were kept, and Pusong cut off their tails and drove the cattle to his home. He then stuck their tails back in the mud back in the king's field. He ran to the king, crying that the cows had drowned in the mud hole.

When the king saw the tails in the mud, he felt very sad. But soon the king heard the truth. Furious, he had Pusong captured and closed inside a cage. The king planned to have the cage thrown into the sea the following morning.

Later that same day, a man walked by to hear Pusong wailing inside the cage. The man asked what was wrong.

"I am being forced to marry the king's daughter," Pusong answered. "I do not want to be a prince!"

Believing that he would be rich if he married the king's daughter, the man offered to trade places with Pusong. They exchanged clothing, and the man took Pusong's place inside the cage.

The next morning the cage was thrown into the sea! A kind fisherman saved the man, but the cage sank beneath the waves.

That afternoon, Pusong strolled past the palace, whistling with his hands in his pockets. The king couldn't believe his eyes. "What are you doing here?" he shouted.

"I came back from the bottom of the sea," Pusong answered. "I met all sorts of wonderful people there, and they sent me to give you their greetings. Your relatives are among them, living in beautiful houses under the water."

The king wanted to see his relatives, like Pusong had done, so he had himself locked in a cage and thrown into the sea.

And that is how Juan outwitted the king and became king himself!

Check In What qualities did each trickster have in common?

Discuss | Information and Ideas

1. What connections can you make among the three pieces in *Many Cultures*? How are the pieces related?

2. Pick one key piece of information that is presented in each of the selections within this book. Explain why you think this information relates to the theme of *Many Cultures*.

3. How have different groups influenced life in the United States?

4. In what ways do you think the writer's personal connection affects her opinion in "Lion Dances and Dim Sum"?

5. Which trickster tale did you like the best? Why?

6. What do you still want to know about cultural traditions from different places around the world?